# CAMPFIRE TALES

# CAMPFIRE TALES

## By Jerry Fearing

NODIN PRESS

ISBN: 1-932472-91-2
Library of Congress Control Number:  2009926254

Design by John Toren
SECOND PRINTING

Nodin Press, LLC
530 N 3rd Street,
Suite 120
Minneapolis, MN
55401

# TABLE OF CONTENTS

# ODE to the OLD CAMPER

By Jerry Fearing

Here's to the old camper. He's the one favoring his aching back as he paddles the BWCA. His are the stiff legs that turn to rubber on the first 180-rod portage. The spirit's willing, but the bones and muscles lack enthusiasm.

He carries pills for his backache, blood pressure and asthma, plus vitamins A through E. To warm his bald head he wears a wool cap to bed along with flannel PJs. When he's finally asleep, his snoring can drive away all wildlife in a 5-mile radius.

DOWN BAG

FOAM PAD

AIR MATTRESS

# Foreword

When campers gather around the fire at the end of a long hard day, they're likely to start swapping stories about adventures and mishaps they've experienced on other trips. Stories about storms, about bears running off with the food pack, or tipped or punctured canoes. It may be a tale of endless days of rain or snow, or of lakes teeming with fish, or the time when the fish simply wouldn't bite and the woeful campers were reduced to their last cup of rice.

I myself have stayed up late around a campfire on many such occasions, telling and listening to yarns. And it occurred to a friend and me that it would be fun to collect a few of these stories and put them into a book. We might even include a chapter on how to survive a camping trip. We asked a number of fellow campers to jot down their best stories and send them to us, then sat back waiting for the stories to come rolling in. But they didn't come rolling in! It seems no one was willing to bother writing down their camping yarns. We prodded one or two in an effort to get things moving, but eventually gave up. The book layout and cover were filed away and forgotten.

More recently, having reached that point in life when there are far more past events to remember than future ones to plan, I decided to transfer some of the reels of old 8mm films that I shot on early camping trips to DVD discs. My thought was that if I didn't save them in this more convenient form they'd just end up in a dumpster when I've gone on to that last long portage.

As I watched these old films I became aware, for the first time, of how often the campers pictured weren't having all that much fun. They were usually tired, wet, and cold, and more than occasionally they were also being chewed up by black flies, ticks, and mosquitoes. So why did we keep going out on those trips, sometimes two and three times a year? Why would anyone leave the pleasures and comforts of home and family to be overworked and miserable? Clearly all the hardship and misery was accompanied by a payoff of some sort.

I'm guessing that the answer is to be found in those stories that we used to tell.

When I refer to "camping" on these pages I mean putting your tent up off the beaten path. We preferred a trail that was less traveled. In the BWCA we'd study the maps looking for a distant, out-of-the-way lake which took a number of long portages to reach, in the hope that when we got there we'd find a quiet, unspoiled camping site. In the Arctic we'd look for an interesting area, often one suggested by a bush pilot or wildlife official who knew the country. Then we'd find a plane that would get us there and come back for us on a given date.

I was always eager to pack up my sleeping bag and head north at the first opportunity. Perhaps it's in the genes. Ages ago, when I was working as a newspaper cartoonist on the *St. Paul Pioneer Press-Dispatch,* an elderly gentleman who was doing a genealogical study of his family tree wrote to tell me he'd come across an ancestor of mine who'd served as a hunter and guide at Fort Snelling in the early 1820's. Then again, it may simply be the result of having grown up along the Mississippi River. I spent my youth swimming, fishing and exploring the then-wooded river banks.

Whatever the reason, I've never felt like an intruder in the woods. I've been comfortable and at home there as much as any of the wildlife.

And I've always enjoyed being there, despite the wet, the cold, and those damn bugs.

I'm going to share some of my camping stories that never made it into that long forgotten book of ours. Come with me on a few of these wilderness wanderings and along the way maybe we can figure out what it is about this camping thing that appealed to my friends and me.

# CAMPFIRE TALES

"... our dream craft wouldn't carry us as far
as South St. Paul."

# 1 The First Camping Trip

My first memories of home are of a little house across the road from the Mississippi River in St. Paul, Minnesota. The community in which we lived, near the high bridge that crossed the river, was called the Upper Levee. In those days the neighborhood was dominated by Italian families, though in earlier times it had also been home to Polish and Czech immigrants, most of whom worked on the railroad. My maternal grandmother raised ten children alone there after the death of her husband; she was the last of the Polish still living on the levee. Our house was just across the fence from Grandma's house.

The levee was an unusual place to grow up in. The streets were lined with well-kept frame houses, each with its own carefully tended garden. The neighborhood had its own grocery stores and saloons. Bocce ball tournaments were held up and down the streets every Sunday in the summertime, with neighbors lined up to cheer the players on. Most men had a boat tied up somewhere along the river.

For us kids the river was our playground—the place where we swam, fished, and built our tree forts and rafts. Even after my family moved up the hill to West Seventh Street when I was about eight, I still spent a lot of my time on the river, building rafts and boats that would carry my pals and me to New Orleans. We had no idea how far that was, or what lay between St. Paul and that distant Gulf city. All we kids knew was that's where the river went and we planned to ride along.

The boats we worked on were usually found discarded on the river bank or in someone's wood pile. We built rafts from logs and boards we scrounged. After weeks of hammering the boats back into shape and tarring the seams, or tying and nailing a raft together, we'd launch them, only to find that our dream craft wouldn't even carry us as far as South St. Paul.

During those childhood years along the river, my friends and I learned a form of camp cooking. Our mothers canned things like tomatoes, beets, pears, peaches, jams, and relishes, and we could always get away with a jar of this or that, along with some bread and a weiner or two. The whole works were thrown together and cooked up in a coffee can over an open fire. It was a kind of "hobo cooking" that we thought tasted pretty good.

At that time wooded areas were always close by, even in the city. I recall spending many afternoons hunting squirrel and rabbit with a sling shot on the tree-covered grounds of the Jim Hill Estate, below the Cathedral Church in the heart of St. Paul.

As a youngster my heroes were people who traveled to what were then the unexplored parts of the world—people like Frank Buck and Martin and Osa Johnson. For some of you youngsters I'll explain that Frank "Bring 'em Back Alive" Buck was a jungle animal collector who wrote books about his adventures in Africa. He went on to put together several movies. I watched them at the old Garrick Theater in St. Paul, and at the time I thought they were the most exciting films ever made. They consisted for the most part of wildlife footage that Frank had shot on his safaris, to which a paper-thin narrative thread was added—things like Frank being crushed by a giant snake, only to be saved by his faithful gun-bearer, who arrives in the nick of time to unwind the thing. I remember one film in which Frank was blinded by a spitting cobra while deep in the jungle. Corny stuff, but I thought it was great.

Martin and Osa Johnson were also African adventurers of that period. They were the first to use color film and record sound on their safaris, which were turned into documentaries about the wildlife of Africa—an early forerunner of the nature shows we so often see on public television today.

These were the people I enjoyed reading about and that filled my dreams with exciting wilderness adventures.

In those early years we spent so much time outdoors playing along the river that we never gave much thought to actually going camping. My first attempt at anything along those lines happened when I was about eight or nine years old. I'm not sure how it came about, but I suspect my mother must have convinced my father to take me and my cousin Joe, who was a year or two older than me, on a father-son outing. (That was long before anyone dreamed up the term "quality time.")

I'm sure the thought of spending a week with a couple of kids in a tent didn't appeal to my father. In fact, I doubt if he had ever *been* camping before that (or after). However it came about, Joe and I found ourselves off on a camping trip with my dad! He'd borrowed an old canvas tent, and a friend drove us out to a lake. I don't think I knew the name of the lake even then. I do remember we were on a gravel road and Dad put the tent up (with great difficulty) at the water's edge. There was a farm up the road a ways where he was able to borrow a boat and buy some fresh milk.

We fished that first day but didn't catch a thing. Later, when we kids went in swimming, Joe and I came out of the water covered with more than our limit of leeches! We sat outside the tent sprinkling salt between our toes and on our legs to dislodge the blood suckers. Despite this unpleasant wildlife encounter, we felt we were having a pretty good time. We didn't even notice the clouds that began to gather to the west of us late in the day. Soon after dark the storm struck. We were terrified as we huddled in that old tent. Lightning flashed, rain poured down, and the wind buffeted the tent from side to side. Suddenly the tent took off in a great gust of wind and we were left huddled in the downpour wearing only our shorts.

Dad shouted for us to grab a blanket and follow him. He led us across the road to a shed in a nearby field that we could see in the flashes of lightning. We were a mess when we got there, covered with scratches and soaking wet. The roof leaked like a sieve but there was an old truck parked inside and we three climbed into the front seat for shelter. We soon realized the truck stank to high heaven: It was littered with dead minnows. Apparently it was used to haul bait, as well as all kinds of waste for use as fertilizer. Joe and I complained loudly about the smell, but we weren't about to go out into the storm, and we all finally fell asleep.

Morning broke bright and sunny. We hurried down to the campsite to round up our clothing. Most of our food was ruined, but we found our tennis shoes and clothes. Even the tent was there, draped over a bush. Dad walked down the road and apparently found a farm with a telephone, for by early afternoon his friend showed up with a car. We packed up the tent and what was left of our soggy belongings and went home.

That was my first camping trip. My father apparently decided this wasn't for him, and never tried again, but I thought it was pretty exciting and my friends and I continued to enjoy our own brand of camping along the river.

"My introduction to wilderness camping..."

# 2 From Korea to the St. Croix

Iwas introduced to *wilderness* camping in 1950, when I was stationed in Korea as a rifleman with the U.S. Marine Corps. Soon after landing at Inchon in October, my unit marched off into the mountains of Korea to drive out the bands of North Korean soldiers who were hiding there. It was fall, and as we moved through the colorful forests and mountains I soon discovered that I was enjoying the camping experience. We were supplied by air drops and operated with a minimum of military restraint. Despite an occasional fire fight as we forced the enemy to move north, there was plenty of time to appreciate the beauty of the countryside. This was my first taste of what I would call wilderness camping. I made up my mind that if I made it back home in one piece, I was going to search out and do some camping in the wild, beautiful places of my own country.

I did make it home but it was quite a while before I got around to trying my hand at camping again. Oh, we made trips to the lake for the opening of fishing season, explored the North Shore of Lake Superior, and visited many of the out-of-the-way small towns in Minnesota. But I did not do any *bona fide* camping for a few years after returning to civilian life.

By 1958 I was married and had two little girls. We knew of a quiet undeveloped park north of St. Paul on the St. Croix River called O'Brien Park. It was easy to interest the girls in a camping trip and I assured my

19

wife it would be fun. So, one Friday afternoon in late summer, we loaded up the station wagon with a tent, food, and sleeping bags and set out for the nearby park. When we arrived we were the only campers in the place.

While I set up the tent and got a fire started, my wife took the girls for a walk down to the river. When they returned we found our four-year-old had managed to get a sap-covered pine cone securely wound up in her hair. It had to be cut out, leaving an unsightly bald spot on the back of her head. (So far, so good.)

Supper went well. The kids liked cooking their own hot dogs over an open fire and enjoyed the buttered ears of corn wrapped in aluminum foil and baked on the coals. After dinner we quickly ducked into the tent to escape the mosquitoes and the rain that was just starting to fall.

We had returned all the left-over food and goodies to the car, so the raccoons that scurried about once we'd gone inside the tent found little to get into. Just before dawn, our three-year-old woke up crying! The corn had passed through her in a torrent, coating her Dr. Dentons right down to the toes. By flashlight we cleaned her up as best we could, dressed her in warm, clean underclothes and zipped her back into the sleeping bag. I sloshed down to the river where I squatted in the rain, rinsing out her pajamas.

After a breakfast prepared in the rain, my wife moved the kids into the car and strongly suggested we go home! So, heedless of the downpour, I valiantly rolled up the tent and somehow got the soggy mess into the wagon. We headed home from the first and last camping trip I would ever make with my wife. It was abundantly clear that camping wasn't everyone's idea of a fun time.

This fact became even clearer to me on subsequent canoe trips when, paddling past a church or scout group, I would notice a couple of small forlorn victims standing at the water's edge with a look that said, "Get me out of here, I want to go home!"

On the other hand, that first experience didn't seem to bother my daughters one bit. In the years that followed I made many camping trips with my children and we always had fun, despite whatever problems nature threw our way. Now that they're grown and living in different parts of the country, they still enjoy hiking and camping.

**"...cooking their own hotdogs over an open fire."**

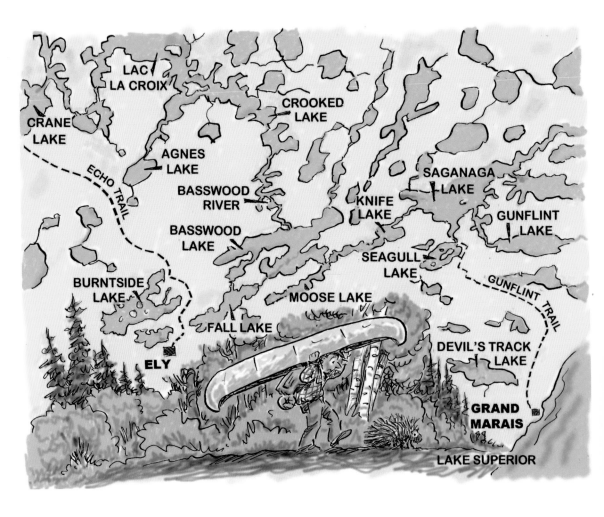

# 3 Discovering the BWCA

As the family grew larger, with three kids and finally four, we continued to enjoy our vacation outings, but to my wife's relief, they were limited to stays at rented lakeside cabins and day-long hikes along the Minnesota and Mississippi Rivers in the vicinity of Old Fort Snelling.

At that time the area had not yet been refurbished and developed into a historic site, and the heavily-wooded bluffs, nestled between two bustling cities, seemed like our own private park.

It never occurred to me in those days to drive up north to camp in the Boundary Waters Canoe Area along the border between Minnesota and Canada. Though I was well-acquainted with rafts and river boats, I'd never spent much time in a canoe.

My introduction to canoe country came about pretty much by accident. Al Lewin, a friend who worked with me at the *Pioneer Press*, was writing a piece about the St. Paul Hiking Club. They were doing a ten-mile hike on Sunday and he asked me to come along for support. On the walk I visited with several of the hikers. One of them, a gregarious older fellow named Walt Jones, was staggered to discover that although I enjoyed camping, I had never been to the Boundary Waters! He insisted on taking me up there to show me around.

It sounded like a great idea so I talked my friend Chuck, a guy who loved to fish, into coming along. Walt had a seventeen-foot aluminum canoe, a motor, and a tent. All we had to bring were extra clothes, sleeping bags, and some grub. I also brought along a one-man backpacker's tent.

And that is how, in the summer of 1963, the three of us jammed into Walt's overloaded canoe and set out up Moose Lake toward the BWCA, riding about three inches out of the water. We sped into Basswood Lake, fishing along the way, then made the 340-rod Horse Portage to the Basswood River and continued north.

A retired over-the-road truck driver, Walt was a robust fellow with boundless energy. He was determined to show us as much of the BWCA as he could cram into ten days. At dawn each morning he was up shouting for us to rollout. "Up and at 'em boys, we've got a lot of water to cover and a couple long portages before dark!" Luckily we had clear weather. In fact,

it was actually hot. Some afternoons were so warm we stripped to our shorts.

Walt turned out to be quite a character. After years of long lonely rides in his truck, he was so happy to have company that he never stopped talking. When he wasn't talking he was singing or telling a joke, (often the same one a number of times). He was delighted to have us along to share the wilderness area he was so fond of. My one-man tent proved to be a blessing. Chuck and Walt shared the big tent. And as I fell asleep each night I could hear Walt going on and on late into the night, sharing his stories and jokes with Chuck, his captive audience.

Despite the heat, Walt insisted on carrying as much or more than Chuck and me on the portages. We felt we had to slow him down a bit and tried to convince him to take it easier. We told him if he broke a leg or had a heart attack, we'd never be able to lug him back across all those portages! Now that I'm past his age myself, I realize Walt wasn't trying to impress us. He was just proving to himself that he could still do it.

This trip was my introduction to the BWCA, and despite the pace set by Walt, I was hooked. I knew I had found my home away from home and was confident Walt had taught us in those few days all we needed to know about getting along in canoe country.

The following spring Chuck and I returned with a rented canoe and a borrowed motor (but without Walt). We invited a teenage cousin of mine to join us. This time we put in at Fall Lake and worked our way up to Basswood Lake. Again we made the long portage and followed the river. It soon started to drizzle and continued raining intermittently for a couple of days, but it didn't bother us much since fishing was good and we were equipped with raingear. This being just our second canoe trip, we didn't know enough to pay attention to the rising water level as we portaged from lake to lake.

Finally, early on a gray, drizzly morning, we set out to retrace our route back to civilization. We soon became aware of a change. The rains had turned what had been swift-flowing but managable water into roiling rapids. As we neared Basswood Lake, we carelessly plunged straight across the currents between Wheelbarrow Falls and Lower Basswood Falls, heading for the shorter portage that lies between them. (We'd crossed it on our way in without a problem.) I'd just finished shooting some film of the falls from the front of the canoe and was slipping the camera into the camera bag when the canoe suddenly flipped over! We scrambled back to the surface and began to work hard in our heavy water-soaked clothes and boots, trying to flip the water-filled canoe right side up again. Once we'd succeeded in doing that, we started heaving in packs, cameras, the food sack, sleeping bags, and anything else that happened to float by in the

churning water. Then, kicking as best we could, we struggled to guide the canoe to the rocky shore as the river current swept us downstream.

We spent the remainder of the morning and early afternoon wringing enough water out of our equipment so we could repack the canoe. Our wet sleeping bags would be useless if night caught us in the woods! The best bet would be to make a dash for the car parked at Fall Lake. But it wouldn't be easy to reach it before dark. We were already cold and tired, the motor was ruined, and we'd been able to find only one of the canoe paddles along the shore.

It became a race with the night. We didn't stop to rest or eat. Each of us took a turn paddling in the back of the canoe while the other two helped with sticks picked up along the way. Portages were done at a trot, weighted down with wet gear. It was already getting dark when we reached Fall Lake, and pitch black by the time we were half way across. But we could see a small light way off in the distance. We headed for it, and luckily, when we reached it there was the dock, with our car parked nearby.

**"We could see a small light..."**

If he tends to be a little owly, it's because he remembers a time when a deer or bear was all you might meet on a portage. A time when Baggies and twisties didn't litter the landscape, and every birch tree on a campsite wasn't stripped of its bark.

But let him fish that favorite lake at sunset with breakfast on the line, a comfortable camp set up a the song of the loon serenading him. Suddenly, he's ageless. All the aches and pains are forgotten and whatver he endured along the way was worth it.

Fearing

# 4 The Right Companions

When preparing a camping trip, the most important consideration is choosing the right companions. No matter how much you try to get along, there will probably be some disagreements, even arguments, especially when things aren't going well—when you're exhausted, the bugs are bad, or the weather has been against you for days. At such times you don't want to be with someone who becomes morose, a complainer who wishes he or she never came along—a person looking for someone to blame for their misery.

In Korea it was often luck that selected your foxhole companion. And I was lucky. Being a platoon runner I shared a foxhole with a corpsman named Mavis. He was actually with the navy assigned to my Marine unit as our first aid man. Of course, he was known as Doc Mavis. A big fellow from Duluth, Minnesota, with a good singing voice and a vast repertoire of Swedish dialect jokes, he was good company and a reliable, understanding friend. Probably because we were both from Minnesota, the twenty-below-zero cold that swept over us near the Chosin Reservoir in the mountains of North Korea didn't overwhelm us as much as it did some of our fellow Marines from southern states. We survived the winter of '50-'51 without permanent damage. True, we spent more than one night down in the snow, covered with a "shelter half," shivering and clinging to one another for warmth. Worst of all, we weren't able to start a fire for fear the smoke would draw mortar and rifle fire from the North Korean or Chinese troops on the mountainside across from us. These miserable conditions would have been even harder to survive but for the amiable companionship of Mavis.

Through the years I've camped with a number of different people. Among them are four who turned out to be ideal companions, men who could be counted on no matter how difficult the conditions became. One of them was a professional naturalist, a man who seemed capable of walking to the moon and back without tiring. His knowledge of wildlife, plants and geology was only equaled by his sense of humor. Another was also a man of vast outdoor knowledge, a high school science teacher and mushroom expert who had served in WW II and seen much of the world. There was also a newspaper reporter and editor, a very good man who had covered stories all the way to the Antarctic and was always open to a new adventure. The fourth guy was a fellow I've known since high school days. He was a zoo keeper and a naturalist who could hold an audience of kids spellbound with a snake, a stone or a dinosaur bone. Although we went off in different directions after high school, our paths kept crossing through the years.

These four fellows were the ones I could always count on to make a pleasant trip, winter or summer, no matter how tough the conditions became. There were disagreements and arguments and sometimes we didn't have much to say to one another for a day or so. But it always passed.

My children, two boys and two girls, also proved to be good camping companions. As soon as they were old enough to carry their own backpacks and knew how to swim, they were ready for a canoe or backpacking trip.

I like to think of these early years as the golden years of wilderness camping. There were still countless lakes and streams waiting to be explored, with few tourists cluttering up the campsites and portages. It was also a time of few park regulations and restrictions.

At that time camping equipment wasn't as accessible or efficient as it is today. Tents were made of canvas for the most part, and we often cut our own support poles from the surrounding forest and used a lot of stones, stakes and rope to keep them taut. There was no zippered bug screen across the entrance and no screened windows. Our packs were either Duluth packs or army surplus. We carried our food in a duffel bag. There wasn't that much freeze-dried food available then and what there was cost a lot. We had to fill our packs at the supermarket with tea bags, cans of beans, chili, powdered soup and Spam along with packaged spaghetti, oatmeal, cocoa, and pancake mix. Boots could be bought at the army surplus stores. Of course, if you could afford it, you could always find more expensive boots or even have them made at Gokey's, one of the sporting goods stores in downtown St. Paul that served hunters and campers. Another was Kennedy Bros. Arms, which carried everything from canoes to elephant guns. Since I didn't have a lot of extra money for such things, I bought most of my summer and winter camping equipment at Morrie's United Surplus Store in downtown St. Paul. The equipment wasn't fancy or exclusive but it did the job and cost a lot less.

"Get out of here—Leave that stuff alone!"

# 5 Winter Camping

The Minnesota Boundary Waters Canoe Area includes a vast number of lakes, islands, and streams, and I wanted to see as much of it as I could. My friends and I often made two trips a year, and sometimes even three. These were usually short trips using a few days of vacation time.

I was then working for a morning paper. The Sunday edition went to bed around eleven PM on Saturday night. After work I'd pick up my gear and companions and we'd drive the rest of the night up to Ely or Grand Marais—depending on where we were going to start out. Then we'd paddle and portage for most of the day. By the time we set up camp late on Sunday you can be sure we were ready to sleep.

It was on such a trip, after we'd turned in on a warm, quiet evening, that I looked out the tent opening to see a black bear nosing around our packs. We'd hung the duffel bag containing our food between two trees, so there was nothing within reach for him to eat. I shouted, "Get out of here, leave that stuff alone!" He looked over at the tent and decided there was nothing nearby worth arguing about and ambled back into the woods. My two startled companions awoke wondering what was going on? I told them there was a bear out there after our packs! They looked out, saw nothing, and went back to sleep, convinced I'd been dreaming or just kidding around. But I stayed awake a long time, sure that as soon as I closed my eyes he'd be back.

After a number of years of such excursions into the BWCA, it became obvious that the popularity of the region was exploding. When we reached a portage, it more often meant sitting in our canoe, waiting our turn to walk across. And the portages were more often cluttered with plastic bags hanging from bushes, trails littered with items of clothing, plastic bottles and broken equipment. When we finally reached our campsite, we usually spent the first half-hour picking up candy wrappers, twisties, wads of aluminum foil and other assorted litter.

To handle the growing crowds of campers, and the degradation that was taking place as a result of it, the forest service established a new set of rules and regulations. Now we could only set up our tent at designated campsites equipped with an iron grate for cooking and a box latrine out in the woods. Bringing in canned food items was no longer allowed. In the early years we drank and cooked with the water from the lakes and streams, but that was fast becoming a risky enterprise, and we were cautioned to carry in drinking water and boil the water we used for cooking.

I realize these restrictions were necessary to handle the flood of campers wanting to use the area. But for us it put a damper on the wilderness experience we had enjoyed for so many years. In an effort to escape the problems of overcrowding, we often made a beeline for out-of-the-way lakes set off from the main routes by difficult portages. But that didn't always pay off. We sometimes found others had worked even harder to get there ahead of us. A better solution was to go up earlier in the spring or later in the fall. Fishing was usually better at those times and we had our pick of campsites. Late fall was the most beautiful and best because by then the mosquitoes and black flies were gone, along with most of the tourists.

We'd been going up later and later each fall until, in the 1960's, the thought occurred to us: Why not go all out and make it a winter camping trip?

After all, I'd survived (and at times even enjoyed) camping in the mountains of Korea in the winter with worse equipment and no experience.

On our canoe trips we often stopped for supplies and equipment at Canadian Waters Outfitters in Ely, Minnesota. We'd gotten to know the owners, Jon and Dan Waters, well enough to ask if they'd be interested in trying some winter camping? The idea appealed to them since the regular camping season would be over by then and they'd have the time. And if it proved practical, they could expand their business to include outfitting winter campers.

Their business contacts with suppliers proved helpful. We found ourselves testing some of the new winter equipment on our trips. For instance, we tested the first plastic snowshoes. They seemed like a good idea and looked real neat. But when we tried to use them at -20° they snapped like twigs! We were also given some of the early down-filled clothing to wear (more on that later). We used primitive snowmobiles to carry our gear across the frozen lakes. (In those days they had to be started with a pull rope like a lawn mower.) Once the snowmobiles had been standing out on the ice all night, we had to take them apart and warm the parts by a roaring fire to get them started again.

It got very cold on our first trip! I had a sleeping bag I'd bought at Morrie's United Surplus. It was the same kind of mummy bag the Marine Corps had given me in Korea. They called it a "down" sleeping bag, but I suspect it was filled, for the most part, with chicken feathers! Yet it did help get me through many a cold night.

There was no stove of any kind in our little tent, but I was smugly confident I'd out-smarted Old Man Winter! I had one of those little metal hand warmers you filled with lighter fluid. I lit the wick, replaced the cover, put the devise in its small flannel sack, and placed the thing, sack and all, in a sheepskin mitten which I then placed on my chest. My face poked out the opening of the mummy bag wrapped funnel-like in a towel. Let the winter winds blow!

My companion wasn't so lucky. He couldn't get his boots off because the felt liners were frozen to his boots, and rather than risk frostbite, he decided to keep stomping around until he thawed them out enough to pull them off. As long as he kept moving, his bulky down parka kept him warm. So, as he marched back and forth in front of the tent he kept me appraised

of what was going on out there. He described the black sky, the thousands of glittering stars, the wolves he could hear howling in the distance, the sound of what must have been a moose going through the thicket down by the point. I finally dozed off listening to his patter.

Suddenly I bolted upright in my bag! I was in pain! The hand warmer must have slipped out of its sack and the mitten while I slept, and come to rest against the inside of my left arm! As I sat up the hot little devil fell in my lap! When I rolled on my side it ended up against my butt! With one hand I desperately yanked at the sleeping bag zipper, while with the other I tried to grab what felt like a hot coal dancing around in there with me. When I prepared for my night in the sleeping bag I'd removed my thermal underwear top but kept the bottoms and my heavy socks on. So the only real damage I received from my runaway heating system was a painful burn on the inside of my left arm. We learned later when we got back to Ely that the temperature had dropped to -50° that night.

As I mentioned, we were trying out some of the new down clothing. The parka of my friend, the zoo keeper, was a honey. It was bright orange nylon and filled with so much down he looked like a balloon with legs. We were snowshoeing across a lake on this very cold day. He'd zipped up his hood so tightly it left only a little peep hole through which to see where he was going. After we'd been mushing along for a while he suddenly stopped and started pulling at the hood! Then I heard his desperate, muffled voice shouting, "Help, get me out of here! I'm roasting!"

His breath had frozen around the peep hole and covered most of the zipper with ice. His body heat had built up in that coat to such a degree that he was sweating profusely. Now, one thing you don't want to do when camping in the cold is get your underclothing wet with sweat. It'll eventually rob you of all your body heat and you'll feel like you're freezing ( and you probably will be). While my friend roasted, I twisted and pulled at the zipper, tying to break away the ice. When we finally got it loose he pulled the coat off and stood there with sweat running down his face, steaming like a lobster that had just been pulled from a boiling pot.

Later on that trip, we all had to deal with another bad situation. We'd left our snowmobiles on the lake and snowshoed into an area where motor vehicles were not permitted. We worked pretty hard getting through the snow to shoot pictures of a beautiful waterfall surrounded by mist and ice. Hurrying back along the shoreline to the snowmobiles, one of our group went through the ice, getting wet to his waist. The question was, do we start a fire there and try to dry him out, or hurry on to the snowmobiles and get him back to camp, where there'd be a fire and dry clothes waiting?

We decided to make a run for it. When we got back to camp he pulled off his ice-encrusted clothing in front of the fire as we rushed about gathering wood to build it up. Since we were all sweating by then from the exertion of rushing back to camp, we gathered around the blazing fire, stripped off our damp socks and long johns, and hurriedly dressed in dry clothes from our packs.

The problems faced on that first winter camping trip were not that serious, and we were confident we'd learned from our mistakes. So we decided to make it a yearly event. And we did get better at it, though old man winter did everything he could to let us know who was in charge.

Men came from out of state to join the crackpots who went camping in mid-winter. There was even a photographer who came along to shoot pictures for a snowmobile commercial.

After losing touch with half our group in a blizzard and later having a snowmobile go through the ice, the idea of encouraging novice campers and outfitting them for winter camping in extreme cold didn't seem like such a good idea.

Even more so than summer camping, there's no doubt winter camping isn't for everyone. This is definitely a young person's sport. As I've drifted into middle age the thought of sleeping on the hard frozen ground, of crawling out of a warm sleeping bag to face a snow-covered sub-zero world

just doesn't hold that much appeal. I've done it and had fun proving I could do it. Now I'd rather stay cozy warm at home watching my DVD's of those winter camping trips.

I recall a comment made by my sister as she watched a film I'd shot of snowshoeing along the snow-swept, ice-encased shores of Lake Superior. She turned to my wife and said, "Save these pictures, If you ever want to have him committed, just show 'em this!"

But I don't want to leave you with the impression that winter camping doesn't have its good points. For instance, there are no bears, mosquitoes or black flies to harass you. Because there's no foliage, wildlife can be observed a long way off, and the tell-tail tracks left in the snow will let you know if a fox, wolf or moose has moved past your camp during the night. You can carry more equipment with you since it all rides in a banana sled that you pull on snowshoes, cross-country skis, or on a snowmobile.

My favorite luxury was a heavy iron pot with a lid called a Dutch Oven. It was ideal for cooking up beef stew, chili, or ham and pea soup, which could be frozen into bricks at home, wrapped in foil and carried in a pack. The kettle simmered on a cook stove or in the coals of a wood fire. We enjoyed colorful displays of dancing northern lights the likes of which could never be seen close to the lights of the city. Then there's the solitude! No one else for miles, just you and your friends sitting next to a warm fire listening to the wolves howling at a black velvet sky.

After a few years of winter camping adventures, I discovered an even more exciting area in which to camp—an unspoiled wilderness with great fishing, plenty of wildlife, and few if any tourists! I discovered the Arctic tundra!

# 6 Arctic Camping

Isn't it interesting the way fate takes us by the hand and leads us along through life? We delude ourselves into thinking we're in charge of planning our future—I'm captain of my ship, right?—when in fact it's the winds of fate that determine where we're going.

If it hadn't been for the chance meeting with Walt Jones on that Sunday afternoon would I have ever paddled off into the BWCA to start a lifelong fascination with wilderness camping? From then on, one thing just naturally led to another. All I had to do was answer the door when opportunity knocked. And the knock usually came at the best possible time!

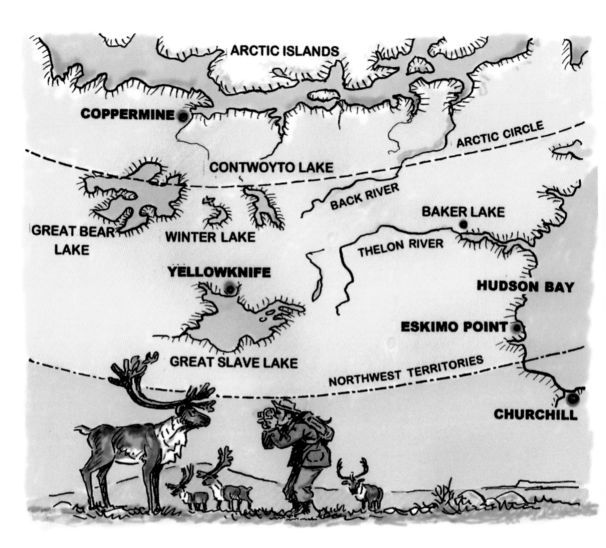

As I mentioned, winter camping had started to lose its appeal. My camping buddies and I were looking for a new challenge.

The office next to mine at the newspaper was occupied by our business editor. He was a man of many talents and wide interests, one of which was part-ownership of a fishing lodge on the Arctic Circle. They flew well-heeled fishermen from all over the country to the lodge to be pampered with good food, comfortable accommodations, and the best fishing in the world. I asked him about camping in the area. "No one goes up there to camp," he told me. "These guys fish all day, come back to the lodge to eat, have a couple drinks and play cards."

Camping in such a remote area seemed like a pretty exciting idea to me. He agreed to include me and two companions on the next flight to the lodge if we made ourselves useful by loading and unloading luggage and supplies along the way. Once there, we'd rent a boat and motor, buy supplies from the lodge, then go off to spend a week exploring the north shore of Great Bear Lake.

All went as planned. My two friends (the newspaper editor and the zoo keeper) and I arrived with a planeload of eager fishermen on the sandy shore of Great Bear Lake. We loaded the luggage and supplies onto smaller pontoon planes which shuttled us all to the lodge. The following morning we left, heading north with a good map, a full box of grub, a couple drums of fuel, a motor, and a good size boat, which we later learned was the lodge's garbage scow. We assured them we'd be back in a week to catch the flight out. They'd also sent along a small hand-held walkie-talkie type radio with which we were to call the lodge in case of an emergency. But as soon as we put an island or two between us and the lodge it was useless.

Making our way through the many islands to the north, we three suddenly felt very much alone in the world. We were surrounded by hundreds of miles of rocky beaches and brush-covered hills on which we believed few, except possibly Indians, had ever camped, with thousands of miles of largely uninhabited lakes and tundra beyond.

The lodge sent along some steaks in the food box. It was best to eat them before they spoiled, so we didn't fish the first day or so. But when we did start fishing for food we found we were in fisherman's heaven! Our routine was to set up camp in the early evening, then take the boat off shore a few feet and catch our supper. It never took more than two or three casts to get a strike. We became very choosy. We kept only lake trout of around six pounds. Smaller ones were more work to clean and bigger ones were more than the three of us could eat at one meal.

A couple days into the trip I discovered we weren't really alone. As we passed a small bay, we spotted smoke rising from a couple of tents located back from the beach. The question of who these people were was answered the next day when a pontoon plane taxied up to the beach at our camp site. It was carrying supplies for prospectors who were working in the area. We told the pilot it wasn't us, but he'd probably find the guys he was looking for a couple miles to the west.

There wasn't a lot of wildlife to see around the lake. Once or twice we heard wolves howling at night and spotted a couple along the beach. Though we didn't see them, the deer and caribou left their antlers scattered about the countryside, letting us know this was part of their territory. Once, while cleaning fish along the shore, my friend the zoo keeper looked up to see a bear sitting in the brush watching him. Leaving the fish he made a hasty retreat back to our campsite.

The beaches were fascinating. Wherever we stopped on shore to make camp or take a break, we ended up filling our pockets with beautiful stones —agates, chunks of petrified wood, crystal and quartz. We finally had to throw most of it back because there was no way we could carry all those souvenirs out with us. The boat was already crowded with chunks of crystal and three sets of Caribou antlers!

One near-disaster occurred a couple days into the trip. While roaring along at a pretty good clip on the north shore we turned into a small bay. Suddenly the motor hit a huge rock hidden below the surface. The cowling that covered the top of the motor flew into the air, the prop pin was sheared and the propeller was nicked and bent! Luckily the cowling landed face down on the surface of the water and bobbed there until we managed to

paddle over to retrieve it. We had good reason to be concerned. If the motor was shot, how would we make it back across this huge lake to the lodge in time for the flight out? We paddled to shore and went to work on the motor. It wasn't badly damaged. We found an extra pin in the repair kit and were able to straighten the prop a bit. Though with a very noticeable vibration, we were able to continue on our way.

We spotted a white mountain a few miles from the lake which piqued our curiosity. Could there still be snow around this late in the year? It wasn't likely. Maybe it was a great hill of white sand?

We decided to pull in and backpack crosscounty to find out what we were looking at. It was hard going. The brush was thick in the draws and the black flies found us as soon as we got away from the lake. When we reached our objective, we were amazed to find it was a mountain of quartz. Well, quartz is often found in conjunction with gold! As we climbed to the top we wondered if this was what those prospectors were looking for. Were we the first to discover it? At the top we were again reminded we were not as isolated as we imagined. There, amid a clutter of rusting sardine cans, was a claim stake with a date and number written on it, along with a metal identification tag. So much for our being the first to discover the white mountain.

All in all, it was a marvelous camping trip. We had a little rain one afternoon. The insects were troublesome only when we ventured crosscountry or up one of the smaller rivers that flowed into the lake. We made it back to the lodge in plenty of time for the flight out. The fishermen treated us like returning heroes. They wanted to hear all about our adventures in the wilds. They may have had great fishing but I suspect we had a much more interesting time.

I'd finally found the campers Valhalla, the last frontier on the North American continent. Back home, we immediately started planning another trip to the land of the tundra. But this time we wanted to meet the people who made their home there—the Eskimos! (I realize the name Eskimo has now been replaced by the term Inuit, but in the '60s and the early '70s, when these trips were made, the accepted term was Eskimo, and I think it right that I use it here.)

This time the business editor couldn't help us. We were going to have to wing it on our own. And again fate was on hand to help us along.

In August of 1969, the naturalist, the editor and I flew to Yellowknife, the capital of the Northwest Territories, located on the north shore of Great Slave Lake. We had no connections there or even much of an idea

as to where we'd go when we got there. The weather closed in after we arrived, so nobody was going anywhere. We roamed around town talking to the bush pilots who operated from there. We met a ranger who'd just returned from a tour of the area north of Yellowknife. He told us about a small group of Eskimos who made their home on Contwoyto Lake. They still lived in the old way, using dog sleds in winter and fishing from skin-covered kayaks in summer—the kind of people we wanted to meet! When the clouds finally lifted a bit we talked a young English pilot into flying us to Contwoyto Lake. I can't recall the exact cost. It seems to me we each kicked in about 200 bucks to charter the pontoon plane for a round trip. In the late 60s that was a lot of money for a working stiff.

It was a hairy flight. We ran into rain and drizzle as the overcast skies thickened. When we arrived at Contwoyto, (how did the pilot know that was Contwoyto Lake—the country was covered with lakes that all looked alike?), he flew over a small group of four or five square white tents nestled in a bay, then headed out to land in the middle of the lake. We had to climb out on the pontoons to paddle the plane to shore. The pilot explained he wouldn't taxi the plane in to shore for fear of damaging a pontoon on unseen rocks.

We unloaded our gear and agreed to meet the plane on that beach in eight days for the flight back. As he flew off, the gamble we were taking started to sink in. That pilot was the only one in the world who knew where we were and when we were supposed to be picked up. We'd have to survive any sickness or serious injury, including heart attack, appendicitis, or broken bones until the plane returned!

We quickly set up camp and made ourselves comfortable. Luckily we'd brought along a small camp stove. There was no wood around for fires. This was early August—late fall in that part of the world. A cold rain or sleet fell almost daily. The ground was sealed by permafrost so the rain that fell stayed on the surface, absorbed into the deep cushion of moss, lichen and small plants that covered the ground. It was like walking on water-filled sponges. Our leather boots were soon saturated and we had to put the plastic bags that had held our supplies over our socks in an effort to keep our feet dry.

But these inconveniences were far outweighed by the wonders of the place. Small groups of caribou frequently showed up to graze near our tent. At dawn the first morning, one of our party walked down to the lake to fish,

and before I was even dressed he came walking back with a huge lake trout. But fish weren't the only thing on the menu. The countryside was alive with ptarmigan, and they didn't fly from us as we approached, they walked away! So all we had to do was herd them together, and with a well-aimed stone we soon had the makings for a chicken dinner.

After a day or so of taking pictures of caribou and settling into our camp-site, we finally walked across the tundra to the bay in which we'd seen the Eskimo tents. We had no idea how they might feel about strangers showing up at their camp.

As we neared the camp there was a great deal of hubbub as people called from tent to tent and rushed out to look and point our way. A young man of about 19 walked out to meet us. His name, we learned, was James Algona. He spoke good English, having gone to school in Fort Simpson, east of Great Slave Lake in the Northwest Territories.

After we explained we were camping near by, we were made welcome, (though I suspect they found it hard to believe anyone was crazy enough to leave the comforts of home to rough it on the tundra). Coffee and bannock were passed around as we sat cross-legged on the ground in front of their tents. James's grandmother seemed to be the matriarch of the group. She looked ancient, with blue tattoo designs decorating her wrinkled face. As we visited with them she carried on a monologue of her own. Of course we couldn't understand what she was saying, but from the giggles and smiles of the others I suspect she was commenting on these goofy strangers.

We made several more trips to the Eskimo camp. I shot movies there while my friends, both excellent photographers, made good use of their 35 mm cameras. When out hunting in the days that followed, the Eskimos usually stopped by our camp for a cup of tea. They thought it was pretty funny that we picked that particular spot to put up our tent because they'd often seen a bear around there and thought it might be part of his territory! Luckily we never met a bear while camping there. But we wondered, Was it a brown bear or a grizzly in whose backyard we were camping?

James and I became good friends, exchanging letters and gifts through the years. I made a couple more trips to visit with him in various parts of the Northwest Territories.

Unfortunately, with all the oil exploration money flowing into the area, prices sky-rocketed, and it soon became exorbitantly expensive to charter a plane. So we had to make our trips into areas by a less expensive means of transportation. We flew to Coppermine, on the Arctic Ocean, via a commercial flight from Yellowknife. And when we went to Churchill on Hudson Bay we got there on a Canadian train through the roadless wilderness.

Through the years I've made seven trips to the wilderness areas of the Northwest Territory. But as my friends and I grew older and a couple of them passed away, the wilderness camping trips came to an end. In recent years I've lost track of James Algona. My last two letters to him have gone unanswered. It may be he's too busy to write, or maybe he moved out of the area. It could be he's no longer with us.

I still have the old movies shot on those trips. The sprocket holes of the film are worn and chewed up, but the colors on that old Kodak 8mm film are as sharp as they were when first developed. Viewing the DVD's made from those films, it doesn't seem so long ago my friends and I (and later with our kids) were trekking across the barrens wondering what we'd find over the next hill.

"...everything was covered with a blanket of wet snow."

# 7 Hunting Tales

Every trip seems to have its own unique incident that leaves an indelible mark on one's memory. Often it's something that leaves us laughing at ourselves. These are the stories that usually crop up when we're relaxing around a campfire.

Through the years I've taken a number of hunting trips to various parts of the country. This, despite the fact I don't hunt. I just went along to do some camping and shoot movies. On one of these trips, in 1970, with two friends to the outback of Wyoming, we darn near ended up spending the winter there!

It was fall but the weather had been warm and dry—so dry that we were able to drive our truck crosscountry without much of a problem. We were miles from any town or even a road when it started to rain.

We pulled into a grove of cedar and set up our tent, to wait out the wet spell for a day or two. Next morning we woke to find everything covered with a blanket of wet snow! Heavy snow continued all day and the next night. The truck didn't have 4-wheel drive so we were pretty sure it would never make it through wet snow. We had to get back home to our jobs so we couldn't just sit around indefinitely, waiting to see what would happen next.

On the second night of snow we decided to take what we could carry in our packs and walk across the hills for the nearest town. We'd have to come back for the truck and the rest of our gear later in the fall or perhaps in spring. When we stepped out of the tent at dawn, we discovered the weather had turned so cold the ground was frozen. Throwing everything into the truck we took off with one of us standing on the back bumper to add weight to the rear wheels and one walking ahead to watch for snow-covered holes and ditches.

It was slow going but after an hour or two we spotted a gravel road across the next valley. We also saw some antelope off to our left. Since we were so close to the road (we reasoned) why not take time to do a little hunting?

The antelope kept moving around the hill as we followed, never giving the hunters a good shot. Soon the walking became noticeably more difficult. Great clumps of snow and mud were now sticking to our boots. The temperature was rising and the snow cover was melting!

Rushing back to the truck, we sped across the valley toward the road. Just short of it we broke through the frozen crust and sank to the axle in mud. We dug out our axe and started chopping sage brush, which we crammed under the wheels in the hope of getting some traction, but it was useless. We only sank deeper.

We'd just about given up hope when a truck came down the road. We waved it down and the driver agreed to give us a hand. With his truck pulling a cable attached to the front of ours, and us in the mud pushing, we finally got it up on the road. Elated, though cold, wet, and covered with mud, we drove to the nearest town and got a room in the only motel. The proprietor wouldn't give us the key, however, unless we agreed to take off all our wet, muddy clothes outside!

On another hunting trip I had my eight-year-old son along. While our companions were off hunting mule deer, he and I went into the mountains to look around and shoot some movies. On our way back we came down out of the forest onto a grass-covered meadow. This was open range country and at the far end of the clearing was a herd of cattle. It would save us a lot of walking if we could cut across this open area. I told my son we'd keep our distance from the cattle, head for the big black rock on the hill, and from there continue on into the woods on the other side.

As we neared the black rock it lifted its head. It was a bull! This herd was his harem and we were trespassers. As he got to his feet we were already making a hasty retreat back to the woods. Luckily we made it before he came after us. We were happy to take the long way around through the forest back to camp.

"As we neared the rock, it lifted its head..."

# 8 Stayin close to Home

So what do old campers do when they want to think they're having fun being cold, wet and tired? My buddies who are still with us are in no condition to rough it. That's also true of me, though I don't like to admit it. But I still get to spend as much time as I like hiking in the woods.

Again, I was just plain lucky years ago to find an old farm across the road from the St. Croix River in Minnesota on which to settle down.

More than forty years later the kids have all grown and moved on, and as I said, my friends have reached a point in life where they would rather sit around talking about camping than take a hike.

Although I'm not likely to take off for the tundra or go paddling the BWCA, the woods still beckon from just across the road. The flood plain along the St. Croix River is a great area for hiking. It's home to wild turkeys, deer, bear, fox, raccoon, and many types of duck and geese. The forest floor is decorated with wildflowers and mushrooms from spring 'til fall. My canoe is always nearby. When no one is around to help paddle, I have a one-man kayak handy. And just to make sure I don't get too lazy, I have a dog who lets me know twice a day (rain, shine, or snow) it's time to take a walk.

Even close to home I manage to get myself into some interesting situations without trying very hard. I'm thinking of the winter day when I went through the ice on the river. It was late in the day when my dog and I were crossing the river. It had been very cold and the ice was crisscrossed with snowmobile tracks, so I felt confident it was safe. Near the Wisconsin side I stepped on a weak spot which had been hidden by drifted snow. The instant I felt the ice give way I threw myself forward and ended up with my arms and chest extended over firm ice, though I was in the water from the waist down. My dog thought I'd better quit fooling around in the water and tried to coax me out by coming up to lick my face! I shouted for her to back off before the extra weight broke off the ice to which I clung.

At that point, kicking my legs and crawling forward with my elbows, I managed to squirm my way out of the water onto the ice. We then hurried back across the river and through the half-mile or so of woods toward home. When I reached the rail fence where I usually ducked under the top rail, I found I was encased in ice and couldn't bend. I had to lean over the top rail and just let myself fall over. When I managed to get back on my feet I was covered with snow.

You can imagine what my wife thought when she looked out the window and saw me stomping stiff-legged up the driveway like a flocked version of the Frankenstein monster! I had to stand around in the kitchen on a throw rug waiting for the ice to melt before I could get out of my wet clothes.

I've found that dogs are by far the best hiking companions. They're good company, curious, untiring, uncomplaining and completely forgiving. It's been my experience that a dog can always be trusted to let you know when it's time for a hike, regardless of weather conditions. Their better hearing and sharp sense of smell will often point out things you might otherwise have missed.

They can also be a bit of a nuisance. When the kids were still around we often camped down at the river on weekends. Our lab loved to come along. She slept at the foot of the tent near the opening and insisted on making a tour of the campsite every couple of hours, just to be sure all was well. So I had to wake up and unzip the screened opening for her, wait for her to complete her tour, and then let her back in. A few hours later I'd have to wake up and do it all over again.

In the fall of '98 I walked down Bright Angel trail to the bottom of the Grand Canyon. For years I'd wanted to make that hike. From time to time I'd made shorter walks into the canyon but was always on my way someplace else and didn't have time to go all the way down. My son, with my daughter and her boyfriend, joined me on the three-day hike to the bottom and back. It was everything a person could have hoped for—a walk in good weather through the most awe-inspiring scenery in the world.

Yet, I feel it was a mistake for this 68 year old guy to make that trip with those young people. I slowed them up and ended up feeling like a burden. They concerned themselves with my well-being when they should have been enjoying the hike. They insisted on lightening my pack by carrying this or that for me, they worried if I was drinking enough water, they asked me how I felt. Would I like to stop and take a break?

Now that I think about it, that's how Chuck and I felt about old Walt on that first camping trip. We were worried the guy might drop dead on us. So here I was walking in his shoes! It was painfully disconcerting to view myself through their eyes. What I'm sure they saw was a tired old man

**Looking for the next shady spot.**

stumbling along slowly on sore feet, just barely able to keep up.

I still hope to be able to do the Kaibab Trail down the north side of the canyon. But when I do, my companions will have to be closer to my own age. We'll take our time and do a lot of sitting and just enjoying the scenery. Then, after a while, we'll saunter on down the trail, looking for the next shady spot.

Well, have we figured out what it is that compels a person to go off looking for that mysterious something, to leave the comforts of home and go off on a camping trip, when they should be experienced enough to know better? I don't think it's just curiosity about what's over the next hill. It's something deeper, like the thing Lewis and Clark probably felt when they looked at the blank spaces on the map, or the feeling that kept people searching for the Northwest Passage and the source of the Mississippi River. It's the urge that says, "Let's go up there and find out what's on top of that mountain."

Whatever the reason, I guess some will always find it worth the effort to search out nature's hidden places, while others will never understand why they do it.

After all, we're told life is a journey. So, Fate, if you come up with another trip for me, come right over and knock on my door. You'll have to knock a little louder, and it might take me a bit longer to get it open. But I'm still game.